Musings: Poems and Tiny Tales

Sydney Crago

BookLeaf
Publishing

India | USA | UK

Presentation by *BookLeaf Publishing*

Web: www.bookleafpub.com

E-mail: info@bookleafpub.com

ISBN: 9789360947101

First edition 2024

For Mom and Dad

The first one was always for you

ACKNOWLEDGEMENT

My first thank you goes to you, Reader. Thank you for choosing this book. I am honored to be sharing these poems and tiny tales with you.

Thank you to my parents, Lisa and David. I decided over a decade ago that my first book would be dedicated to you. I hope you like it.

To the Sorry I'm Booked crew, Lauren, Mary, Clair, and Kelsey for being the book club I dreamed about having.

To the Unhinged Bozos who remind me most days that we are writers first.

To Meredith and Mark for the memes that make me laugh.

To Luna, bark, bark, bark. (Translation: I love you.)

Thank you to those who helped me make this book better:

Becky, your impressions, your suggestions, and your encouragement over the years have been invaluable.

Hattie, for your kind advice and honest answers, for catching typos, and for reminding me that I can do whatever I want.

Andrea, for always asking for the next story, the
next chapter. I'm sorry I made you cry.
Jake, for reading it and for loving me.

PREFACE

Hello, Reader.

In front of you is a collection of poems and tiny tales.
Each one stands alone. Read them in any order you like.

These pages are filled with childhood memories, teenage angst, college hijinks, and becoming an adult.
These are the stories of artworks that have moved me,
of myths that haunt me,
of moments that made me cry,
of words that inspire me,
of times when I clung to books like a life raft,
of nights when I looked to the stars for answers
of the days when I dreamed of more.
I wrote this collection with my heart, even the parts that have been broken, and the parts that have healed. I wrote about the things that I love, that make me laugh, that remind me to listen, that need to be said.
I hope you enjoy what lies on these pages. I hope you find favorites. I hope you'll tell your

friends about this book filled with stories and phrases that burrow into your brain and make a home there.

More than anything, I hope you find your time reading this book well spent.

Without further ado, I give you Musing: Poems and Tiny Tales.

Take the Tour

Welcome. Take off your shoes, please. We can't make more of a mess than there already is. Remember, no flash photography or video. We thank you for your cooperation.

This is our main computer. It runs logic. Well, it usually runs logic. We've been fighting some viruses for the last decade or so. Can't seem to find the manual, so we make do with what we've got.

Here's our memory banks. Let's see if we can pull a file up. Ah yes, the combination to our high school locker. It probably could be deleted, but you never know when you might need it. Can we pull up the memory of unplugging the coffee pot this morning? Sorry, no, we don't store that data.

And here is our panic alarm. Break glass in case something might go wrong. Please watch your step. We never seem to get all the glass up before the next cause for alarm.

Here's the well of hope. No, I won't send the bucket down. It ran dry ages ago, and we are still waiting for more rain.

That planter over there is where we grow love. We water it with dog kisses and shield its blossoms from the burning sun of comparison. It has been blooming lately; we've finally figured out the right soil for its roots.

These are the caffeine gauges. As you can see we're running low. I'll press the button for another shipment. No, that pounding is supposed to happen. The throbbing pain is how we ensure the next delivery will be quick.

Don't look in that closet. That is where we store the secrets. Where we keep the things we never talk about. Ignore the growling inside. We suspect the shame monster knows how to pick the lock to her cage.

This radio is powered by our song collection. We've got a pretty extensive lyric book. It comes in handy for when we feel like singing. Please don't touch the dial. Sometimes it gets stuck on one song and plays it on a loop. We don't want that today.

Do you have to go so soon? But you didn't get to see the cupboard where we store the tears for sad movie scenes. What about the dream generator? You never know what it will create. Can I tempt you with a fresh scone and a cup of tea from our cafe? It's located in the library of books we've read about distant kingdoms and made-up lands.

Well, if you must go, we understand. Follow the map to the nearest exit, otherwise, you're sure to get lost in the maze of what-ifs and worries. Don't forget to leave us a review and visit again soon.

Eww

Hold my hand atop the syrup-covered diner table where the red vinyl booth is cracking and the waitress still marries the ketchup bottles against health code regulation.
Kiss my cheek while we stand in line for the roller coaster, sweat dripping from our armpits, melting away the sunscreen, sure to leave us crisp and red and peeling.
Say "I love you," as you brush my hair from my face, my body lurching forward over the white porcelain, and every muscle in my body tenses as another gag takes over my throat, too occupied in the act of losing my lunch to say it back.
Wrap your arms around me as I cry into your shirt, pulling me tight against your chest, crushing my nose against the waffle knit, coating you in the wet of tears and snot.
Bring me soup in bed when the cough wracks my chest, my voice is muffled by the pressure in my head, and the scant breaths I manage to take fill my lungs with the aroma of vapor rub.
Whisper that you are mine, and I am yours, while the fear churns through my veins, taunting me with what-ifs, as I beg you to drown out the

lies I tell myself about the rot inside me, about
being too much.
Stay.

Allergies

Do you have any allergies? Check all that apply.

- Trees
- Grasses
- Weeds
- Outside
- Mold
- Dust mites
- Dusting the house
- Cats
- Dogs
- Rabbits
- The Easter Bunny
- Cockroaches
- Guys named Chad
- Bees
- Being honest
- Penicillin
- Latex
- Sex shops
- Peanuts
- Tree nuts
- Deez nuts
- Seafood
- Something brushing your leg in the ocean
- Commitment
- Gluten

Horoscope

The stars twist above her in their preset dance
And she wonders if it is just a pattern to be
decoded,
Like an easter egg left by the creators for
dedicated followers to find.

If she could decipher their movements,
Maybe she'd know when to fold her lousy hand
of cards,
and when to bluff her way to taking the jackpot.

Maybe she'd see the heartaches coming,
Like a wave coming into shore,
and she'd have enough time to run up the sandy
bank
and keep the hem of her dress sleeves dry.

Maybe she would know the plan laid for her,
And sing along to the words of the universe,
Like the lyrics to a song, she's heard a thousand
times before.

Maybe she wouldn't lie awake at night,
looking to the skies for answers that don't exist,
like a child wishing upon a star, when she should
be sleeping.

Overnight: Gallery 224

"Andy's coming," Herbert, the Civil War soldier, yells.

The woman with the red scarf wrangles the toddler in a blue sailor suit onto her lap. The ballerinas are commanded back into posture by the mistress of the studio. The wind ceases, halting the flow of the waterlilies around their pond.

A security guard's hand reaches for the metal handle of the door, pulling it open toward him. The heels of his dress shoes clack against the wooden floor, each step echoing in the empty gallery. Headphones fill his ears with the high, tinny sound of a radio broadcast. Herbert leans forward in his frame, as the guard walks past. He shakes his head, unable to overhear the score of the game. The man, with his driving gloves perched on the wheel of the jalopy, rolls his eyes.

The guard reaches for the handle of the far door and glides through its opening. After a moment, it thuds closed.

"Annabelle!" The ballet mistress shouts. "You call that balance? You were wobbling all over the place!"

"Oh, he wasn't paying attention anyway." The woman in the red scarf scoffs as she releases the young boy from her arms. "Give the girl a break."

"She's had over a hundred years to master that pose, and she still fails. Oy-vey." The mistress strikes her cane against the dance floor. The tutus of the girls bounce as they scurry towards the bar.

"Give it a rest, Babette," the man in the car sighs. "I really can't listen to you yell tonight." He rubs his temple.

"Bah!" The mistress waves her hand through the air. "I don't tell you how to drive, Charlie. You don't tell me how to run my studio."

"What would he know about driving?" The woman in the red scarf laughs. "He hasn't gone anywhere in that thing in the last century."

"Michel!" The man in the car calls.

"I'm not getting into this!" A voice answers from around the corner.

"Michel!" The woman in the scarf yells.

"No!" The voice calls.

"No!" The toddler runs past his mother, repeating his favorite word.

"Plié!" The ballet mistress yells, smacking the tip of her cane against the floor. The ballerinas snap into formation and bend their knees.

"NO!" The chorus of characters yell. The wind whips the surface of the water lilies' pond.

"Honestly," the voice sighs. A creak and a thunk sound from around the corner.

"I knew he'd come!" A blonde dancer says to the young brunette next to her. Both girls smile.

A figure of cast bronze steps into view, taking center stage on the floor of the gallery.

"Michel!" The toddler squeals, as he leans forward, onto the gold-gilded edge of his frame.

"Hello, Paul." He smiles at the boy.

"Hello, Michel." The woman in the red scarf says, sitting down on the grass next to her child.

"Hello, Elizabeth." The brass man meets the woman's eyes. "Causing trouble again tonight, are we?"

"Always, Michel. Always." She laughs.

"You can say that again." The man in the car reaches for the glove compartment. With a turn of a handle, it falls open to reveal a bottle of wine, a flask, and a golden cigarette case with a "C" engraved into its silver surface.

"Drinking and driving are we?" Elizabeth teases. Charlie, the driver, takes a long swig from the flask.

One of the ballerinas drops her hand from the bar and places it on her hip. "I thought you just said he didn't drive!"

"Annabelle!" The dance mistress yells. "Do you
want to stay after class for added reps tonight?"
The ballerina sighs and repositions her feet on
the floor and her hand on the bar.
"She has a point, Babette." Charlie refastens the
lid of the flask.
"Oh, hush!" Elizabeth calls across the gallery to
him.
"Ah-hem!" Michel clears his throat. "Perhaps,
you don't need me for this argument after all."
"NO!" The chorus of voices says again.
"Please?" Herbert says, taking his eyes away
from the door for a moment. "Tell us: Have the
tulips bloomed today?"
A hush fell over the group. Michel smiles. "The
tulips are blooming." He says. Babette takes a
seat on the wooden stool that graced the corner
of the dance studio. The trio of ballerinas behind
her, gracefully, silently, seat themselves on the
studio floor.
"Really?" Charlie cranes his neck toward the
skylight as if the flowers would be visible
through it.
"They are." Michel turns toward the ballerinas.
"They are pink, just like the color of your
dresses."
"Tutus!" Annabelle corrects him as she looks
down at the stiff tulle that circles her waist. Her
fingers trace its folds.

"Right, right." Michel nods. "Now," He plants his hands on his hips. "It's your turn."

The wind whistles through the branches that overhang the branches of the pond.

"Yes, you're right. The new daytime security guard does whistle an awful lot." Michel looks to the pond, which, seemingly satisfied by his attention, returns to a gentle breeze.

"Who's next?"

"I have two things." Herbert takes his gaze away from the door again and looks at Michel. "One, I heard a woman say that the cafe downstairs has started serving something called 'egg bites.'" The soldier lifts his fingers to make a set of air quotes, communicating that the name, though strange to him, was a direct quote. "Two, I heard another woman say that Taylor Swift is releasing a new album."

"She is?!" Annabelle flew up to her feet.

"No way!" The blonde ballerina next to her squealed.

"Girls!" The dance instructor smacks her cane. The girls continue to jump up and down in excitement. The instructor rolls her eyes, seeming to have given up on both their manners and instruction for the evening.

"I heard that, too!" Elizabeth smiles.

"When?" Charlie asks.

"I'm not sure," Herbert answers. "Michel?"

Michel shrugs. "I'll ask around."

"I want answers tomorrow, Michel!" The mistress lifts her finger in a gesture usually reserved for scolding her pupils.

"I'll do my best, Babette."

Herbert returns his gaze to the glass door, his ear turned toward the rest of the group in rapt attention.

"Babette?" Michel asks.

The dance instructor straightens in her chair and clears her throat, taking a dramatic pause before opening her mouth.

"Today, Babette." Charlie rolls his eyes and reaches for the flask in his lap again.

"Quiet," she scolds, "or I won't tell you anything."

"You never do anyway." Elizabeth unknots the red scarf from her neck and drapes it around the shoulders of her toddler, who has come to sit next to her. He yawns as he leans into his mother.

"Nonsense!" Babette scowls in Elizabeth's direction. "I always have gossip to share."

"They call it 'tea' now," Elizabeth taunts the old-fashioned woman.

"Why on Earth would that do that?" Babette scoffs.

"Why do they do anything?" Charlie takes another swig from his flask.

"Honestly, it makes no sense." Babette shakes her head.

"Perhaps," Michel offers, trying to settle the topic, "it is because they share news over cups of tea."

"That must be it!" Elizabeth smiles down at the bronze figure beneath her frame. "You always were the brightest of us, Michel."

"Could you be more obvious?" Charlie teases. "I don't know if the water lilies have caught on yet."

The wind stirs the flowers of the lilies in their pond.

"Don't insult them," Elizabeth laughs. "They understand flirting just fine."

"Do I get to say my piece or not?" Babette interrupts.

"Please." Michel sweeps his hand out in front of him, gesturing to her to take the floor.

"There's a new exhibit moving in downstairs." She leans forward. The rest of the art waits for her to continue. "Tiffany. Glass." She thumps her cane on the hardwood of the dance studio. "Can you believe that?"

Elizabeth gasps and looks from one frame to another. "Does anyone know who is getting the crates?"

The others shake their heads, one by one, turning to look at Michel, whose arms are crossed. "I'll ask about that, too," he says.
"It can't be us!" Babette scoffs. "We're far too popular."
"That's what you said about the Grecian pottery last time," Charlie groans. "They locked half of them away to make room for gowns!"
"I like the gowns!" Annabelle smiles.
"Oh, you would!" Charlie rolls his eyes at the child.
"Charlie, if you can't be kind, you are going to have to drive away." Elizabeth scolds.
"You're not my mother!" Charlie crosses his arms.
"STOP!" Herbert holds up his hand. "He's coming back."
"Go Michel." Babette flaps her hands as if shooing a cat from the room.
"I'll see you tomorrow!" Michel calls over his shoulder, darting around the corner and back to his pedestal.
"Ask about the exhibit!" Elizabeth calls.
"Ask about Taylor Swift," Annabelle says.
"Tell us more about the tulips," Herbert whispers, as he takes up his designated pose.
The security guard reaches for the door's handle.
Outside a songbird starts to sing to the dawn.

Look Up

I call those Toy Story clouds for the way they
are pasted in the sky like the wallpaper in
Andy's room: cotton fluff on Crayola blue,
routine and repeating. Isn't today perfect? What
could you possibly have to complain about?
Who cares that the sun hurts your eyes?

I call that a Turner sunset for the way the hues
flow into each other as if brushed together by the
artist with a preoccupation with dawn and dusk.
Do you think God is commissioning his work
now? Sometimes, I think he must.

I call these cornfield twilights for the way the
sky fills with stars, the way it was when I was
young in a town with no stoplights, where we
spent summer nights by campfires, feeling small
next to the stalks that cast shadows on our
laughter, beneath the blanket of pinprick lights
above. Did you make up new constellations?
Did you name them after your friends?

I call this a gasping moon, for the way it looks
down on you in surprise, mouth open wide, its
crater eyes in shock. I wonder, if it could talk,

would it tell how it presides over the darkness, a
silent sentry, doomed to watch us all make
mistakes we wouldn't dare in brighter light? Do
you think it saw what you did?

Waiting for Them

She ran her fingers over the weave of the blanket. The cement underneath it still contained heat after a full day of baking beneath the August sun. It leached into the muscles of her back, as if to make up for the fact that it was a hard place to lay.

"Are you sure we'll be able to see it from here?"

"Yes." She answered, not taking her eyes from the stars that hung above her, a mobile spinning slowly, attempting to lull the planet to sleep.

"But nothing is happening yet."

"Not yet." She shifted on the blanket making room for the child to crawl into the crook of her arm.

She felt his hair against her bare skin, the heat of his body pressed against her side as he yawned.

"Getting sleepy?"

"No!" He protested. She didn't have to look at his face to know that his nose was scrunched, a look of defiance.

"It won't be much longer now." Her eyes scanned the stars, looking for the patterns she learned in her youth. "Watch the Big Dipper." Her finger raised, tracing the shape.

"Is that where they'll come from?" The boy
asked.
"Maybe," She offered. "It's hard to know."
"What if we missed them?"
"We didn't."
"But, Mom," His voice was high.
"Yes, Honey." Her eyes never left the stars.
"What if we did?"
"Then," she sighed. "We just be thankful we got
to see the stars."
She could feel his head nod against her frame.
His hand laid on her stomach; his forehead
pressed against her breast.
"Why do you love them so much?"
"Because," she smiled. "They remind me that I
am small."
"You're not small." His body shook with
laughter against hers.
"Compared to the stars, I am." She said,
"Sometimes, you need to feel small when the
rest of life feels too big."
The boy nodded, even though he didn't
understand, and turned his eyes back to the sky.

Come Down

Head in the clouds,
They said.

Better than in the sand,
She said.

Square Peg

There is a book on my shelf with your name
scrawled inside, a dedication that you signed
when you presented it. "Your favorite," you said,
between bites of chocolate from a heart-shaped
box, and I thought maybe you meant your
favorite was me.

There is a stack of photos in a shoebox, one that
I never open, tucked away high on a shelf, out of
reach. In them, we pasted on smiles as the
landmarks stood behind us, as I tried to forgive
you for talking over my dreams.

There are tear stains on the carpet, where
mascara streaked the fibers, where I collapsed
mid-hike up the stairs to my bed, where my
heart shattered like a dropped glass, the
fragments glistening with the blood.

There are more days now when the sun shines,
when I can't remember your middle name,
where I can't remember the taste of the flavors
on my tongue in the restaurant we found, where
I don't replay the melody in my memory, where

I forget that your hand signed the check when it came.

But in the darkness, I look to the ceiling and ask the plaster why. The gentle breath of the better man beside me answers, slow and rhythmic, like a clock ticking, sure and steady. I grip his hand tighter. I feel my pulse slow, beat after beat, aligning with mine. The night wraps us both in stillness 'til dawn.

Cheerios

Pull the box from the third shelf on the wire rack
in your tiny kitchen. Set it on the counter you
can reach without moving your square-toed
dress-shoe-clad feet. Hear your wife's hair dryer
whirring down the hall. Look out the window at
the sun peaking over the apartment building next
to yours. There is a potted cactus that sits on the
window sill, opposite your window, in a big
kitchen, with no wire racks and a countertop that
looks like granite.
Sigh.
Reach for the cabinet door with the white,
chipped paint where this week's grocery list is
taped. Remind yourself again to repaint the
cabinets. Pull out a bowl on whose depths
Winnie the Pooh is barely visible after a
thousand washes. Open the cereal box and pour
some on top of Pooh Bear. Listen to them clink
as they pound his plastic face. Hear the suction
release as you swing open the fridge door. Reach
for the two percent milk amongst the
Tupperware containers of leftover pasta,
meatballs, and mashed potatoes. Listen to the
shuffle of the cereal as each piece pushes against
the bowl's sides, forced upward by the rising

milk. Carry the bowl and the box to the table covered in coffee rings and crumbs that you forgot to wipe up after dinner last night. Dip your hand into the paperboard box. Listen to the crinkle of the bag as you pull up a handful of O's.

Stuck.

One is stuck under the leather band of your watch whose hands point out the time: 7:06. Release the O's onto the highchair tray for your teething son. Watch him pull a spit-covered hand from his mouth and paw at the cereal. Tumbling O's plink on the tile as they roll to hidden corners where the broom will never find them. Admire his tiny fingernails, the ones that you watched your wife, so carefully, trim last night, as she sat cross-legged on the living room floor, holding your curly-haired baby in her lap and murmured to him a song with words you did not know to a tune you have heard a thousand times. Kiss the spot of his head that still seems a little soft.

Smile.

Sit down to eat your bowl of cereal. Realize you forgot your spoon.

Overheard

She turned her head to the side, toward the couple in the booth whispering over a shared tray of cubed cheeses, sliced deli meat, and fruit. She lifted the glass of red to her lips, pretending to take a sip. She will nurse it all night, to feed a much more addictive habit.

It started the same way so many conversations do. "So then I said, 'You can't be serious?'" The woman's voice rose over the music piping through the speakers.

"And?" He plucked a grape from the tray.

"He told me to, 'just do it!'"

"Did you?"

"No." Her voice hitched.

"What did you do?"

"I told him to go to Hell," she admitted.

"You did?"

"I did."

"Wow." His shoulders thumped back against the booth's wall.

"He fired me on the spot." The tremble in her voice hung like the final note of a song in the air.

The two women to her right spoke to the bartender.

The first one said, "Can I get a slice of the carrot cake?"

The other followed suit. "The chocolate lava cake for me, please."

"Coming right up." The bartender tapped the order into the terminal's screen.

"Did you hear that Ashley is having a girl?" The first woman lifted her glass from the paper coaster.

"What?"

"I thought you knew!"

"I had no idea!"

"It's their fourth."

"Guess she'll have to get a minivan now." The woman smiled.

"Our parents are thrilled to be adding a grandchild."

"Oh, I'm sure." She nodded along.

"Keeps them from asking me when it's my turn." Anger boiled the last two words.

"Oh, Chelsea." Her friend laid a hand on her shoulder.

"Some day." The woman lifted her glass.

"Until then, at least there are margaritas."

Their glasses clinked together, and they both took a swig.

The bartender whispered to the server, as the glass filled with a dark amber beer,

"Still need a ride after we close?"
"Just a ride?" The server raised an eyebrow.
The bartender smiled, "I don't want to impose."
"With you, it's never an imposition."
"What did you say about position?" She teased.
"Shhh, not here. Not now."
"I'll see you at closing."
The server nodded, setting a round of drinks on
the tray.

She took a tiny sip of the wine in her glass,
determined to keep her tab closed for the rest of
the night.
No one looked in her direction, as she reached
for her phone.
Her finger hovered over the screen, unsure
where to click.
She let it go dark.

Search History of a Single Woman

Margarita recipe
Stream Dirty Dancing
Patrick Swayze IMDB
Ghost release year
Pottery classes near me

Flights to Santorini
Flights to Aruba
Flights to Cancun
Flights to Miami
Cabin rental Lake Michigan

New true crime series
Stream true crime
Netflix sign up
When did Netflix raise price
Create Gmail account
Netflix free trial
Zodiac Killer latest theories

Is speed dating still a thing
Singles meetups
Bars near me
Download Bumble

Lasagna for 1 recipe
How to open a jar
How to open stuck jar
Tricks for opening jars
Pizza delivery near me

How to know if a cut needs stitches
Urgent care near me
How to do self Heimlich
Do I need a will
Beneficiary if no spouse?

Pottery Poetry

The clay slides under her hands,
coaxing the lump into a smooth ball of potential,
before sinking her fingers into its center.

She lets it coat her skin in a fine layer of gray,
making over her hands, a union of sorts,
as she pulls the ridges of its walls into place.

Gently she watches it twist under her fingers,
around and around in a slow dance,
growing under her guidance into a new shape.

She cuts its base free from the wheelhead
and lifts it through the air to a slab of wood,
letting it rest, as it accepts its new form.

When it has dried, she will take the metal
and slice away the flaws of her fingers,
giving the pot an air of grace.

And then, she will cradle her creation,
dunking it into a baptism of color
bestowing upon it a layer of protection.

By fire and time,

it is transformed,
hardened and solid, new and final.

It gets a new name:
vase,
and a purpose:
to be a vessel for beauty,
for flowers given in love.

Pretty

32

The tulips died. Their blossoms flopped over the
side of the glass, stems faded yellow-green,
formerly pink petals stained brown.
I pulled them from their vase, a cut-crystal
vessel still bearing the residue of a sticker that
noted its price at the Salvation Army.
Into the garbage can with the coffee grounds and
tin foil they went, and I wondered if it made me
a bad person, to discard something so pretty, so
quickly, at the first sign of age.

Tell Me

Tell me the truth.
Tell me I'm pretty.
Tell me when your flight lands.
Tell me what you think of this song.

Tell me what you need and how I can help. Tell me where you want to go for dinner. Tell me what you think of my new haircut. Tell me where we are.

Tell me who hurt you. Tell me your secrets. Tell me how you got that scar above your eye. Tell me how you got the scar on your heart. Tell me why.

Tell me the meaning of life. Tell me what jobs I should apply to. Tell me who I should love. Tell me the answer to the riddle from third grade that still keeps me up at night. Tell me why the chicken crossed the road. Tell me when I'll die. Tell me why I should stay. Tell me why I should go.

Tell me what you want. Tell me what time to set an alarm for tomorrow morning. Tell me how you take your coffee so that I'll always know that about you. Tell me how it feels to hold my hand. Tell me that I'm safe. Tell me a lie.

Tell me a story about growing old. Tell me a story about who I'll become when I grow up, when I really grow up someday. Tell me a story about how you'll always remember that time we danced in the living room after midnight, after downing the cocktails I made stronger than planned.

Tell me you want me.
Tell me I matter.
Tell me you'll listen to what I have to say.

Running

"Why do you like running?" He asked.
I laughed like that was the answer.
He tilted his head, waiting for words I didn't
have.

How do I tell him that my heart wants to run to
the mountains where I can gaze at a still lake
reflecting the clouds above? I long for days
spent on foreign shores, running on rocky
beaches to the crash of waves reaching for my
toes. I know the sound of cobblestone steps
under hand-crafted leather sandals, the smell of
fresh bread wafting through the propped open
door of a Parisian bakery, and the sight of
flowering orange trees in the Grecian gardens. I
want hands clutching my fingers in the first light
of dawn as wobbly steps are undertaken by tiny
toes. I ache to lie on the couch with an old dog
with a graying snout where I remember there
was once dark fur after long days on my feet. I
dream of shaking hands with characters in
costume while I stand in line to be amused by
the same rides I boarded as a child. I wish for
summer days spent dashing off to made-up
places as I read the afternoon away in a

hammock. I hope for a day when I can pass a penny on the sidewalk without thinking about the balance in my account. I pray for a hundred more years before my feet are tired of standing in front of canvases in galleries that once were palaces.
And instead, I go running on the roads of our city, because that I can do.

"Because I like it," I say.
He nods like that's the real answer.

Bloom Where Apollo Plants You

"Come back," he called, hand outstretched
toward the nymph, a drop of blood still
glistening on his shoulder.
But she runs faster.
"Daphne!" His heart thumped in his chest in
rhythm with the fall of each foot, crunching
leaves, crushing branches with the sole of his
sandals.
But she turns toward the brook, flowing through
the ravine.
"Please!" He begged, watching her flick a gaze
over her shoulder.
Her cheeks flush red with effort, ringlets of hair
extending in midair, suspended by the speed of
her flight.
"Stop," he called, a command in tone, a plea in
his throat.
But she runs through the water, nearly slipping
on the algae that covers the bottom of the
stream.
"Please," he said.
She falters for a moment, just a hitch in her gait,
the length of an inhale, pulling in the sharp tang

of sweat, his sweat, so close here on the edge of
a sunlit field.
His hand grazed her hip.
The transformation takes hold.
Her skin erupts. His fingers press into her flesh,
hardening under his touch, rough and firm. Her
hair brightens, each strand turning from honey to
moss, sprouting leaves from root to frayed end.
"No," he whispered.
"Ye-" her lips freeze before she can hiss the last
letter.
And in the shade of her branches, he wept.

Providence

I imagine that it was raining on the day he
brushed your final stroke. The drops rolled down
the tiled roof, the inspiration for the final dew
drop he planted on your petals. A spring rain,
full of new life–your life–just beginning. You
were born by the signature of his name upon
you.
The moisture in the air kept your oils malleable
as he walked past you day after day, tempted to
return to your canvas.
Did the boar bristles ever hover over your
surface again while you waited on the easel
those long, final weeks?

The spring rains ceased, and the summer
cemented your un-wilting blossoms. His hands
nailed you into the carved wood of the frame,
sealing you as beautiful with a custom crown.
Upon your investiture, did you ride away in a
carriage, whisked in haste to the mansion of the
artist's patron, a worthy prize for their time, and
their gold, and their faith?
Did you preside over the hallway or hang above
the mantle?

Were you warmed by the flames of a fire
burning or kept pinned to the drafty stone of a
county seat's wall?
Tell me about the eyes who first admired you.
Whose lips dared claim you as "mine"?

Then, a fateful day, when a newly purchased
jewel was carried through the doorway and into
your home. Was she prettier than you? Was her
artist young and talented? They lifted you from
the nail where you stood guard for decades
against the drab, dim, and bland. They stored
you away from the light, in the name of
preservation. Did you know then, that you were
old news?
Did you sense the absence of eyes on your
pigment?
Did you dream of the sun's rays caressing your
lines once again?
And when they removed you, or sold you, or
unearthed you among the forgotten heirlooms,
dated gowns, stuffed game, did they admire your
beauty or take the low bid to be rid of your
frame?

How did you arrive here? By boat? By train?
Did you cross the ocean in weeks or in hours?
Were you stored in a crate for decades?
Centuries?

Did you forget the human face until they
unboxed you from your holding?
Did they use gloves to point to your flaws? Did
they call you beautiful? Did they comment on
your worth? Have they decoded your visage for
hidden meanings, for secrets?
Did they ask you about your artist, the one who
dreamed you into existence?

Am I asking too much of a canvas and paint?

Exhibit Placard

The Letter
Unknown Author
1926
A bequest to the museum by the F. Henry's estate

The letter by an anonymous author was found in the wastepaper basket of the artist's studio. It was presumably torn in half by him and covered in blue paint in an attempt to obscure its contents. The paper would have been bound for a burn barrel, a common practice for the mail of the—usually—secretive F. Henry, had he not succumbed to a heart attack, leaving it for his family to find, and preserving it for us today. Its contents shed a new light on the work that was produced bearing his name. While it remains unattributed, scholars agree that its author is most likely one of his students, a woman whose circumstances prevented her from working under her own name.
The cursive script has been examined through several scientific and analytical means to determine not only the accuracy of the letter's contents but also to narrow down the list of

potential authors. While several names have been eliminated from consideration, a shortlist of potential writers remains.

The contents of the letter read:

My Dearest Henry,
I have buried your last letter, but every word remains etched in my mind. I do this for you, for us, for the work. I saw the way the pen shook in your hands. I know your fear; it is one that we share. You write as if I hold your fate in my hands. I'm sorry to report that all that I hold is the brush. I swear under heaven above that I wield it for you and you alone.
He doesn't know. He thinks I have been taking cooking lessons every Thursday. You'd think he would grow suspicious seeing as I never come home smelling of onion and that water still seems to burn rather than boil under my watch. We know I was never meant to wear an apron in the kitchen, only in the studio.
He has, however, noticed the way that I talk about the light through the tender leaves on a spring morning or the curving lines of the furniture in our home. He is starting to ask questions about the colors that stain my dresses. He asked again yesterday what I was charging on our account at the grocer.

Therefore, I implore you: do not write to me here. Do not stop by the home, even under the guise of bible sales. Sign your name to our florals, and our landscapes, and our nudes. I dare not have you be the reason his fist finds the plaster wall again. The man believes your tutelage of me ended when I took his ring, and so we must guard our meetings like Heimdall defends the bridge, like a bear protects her cubs, like glass saves my favorite image of you from the dust and damp of daily life.

I dare not attend this Thursday next. I fear he may follow me. It's something in his eye, the way they dart to their corners when he thinks I cannot see. Instead, wait for me near the entrance to our park at noon on Monday. If I am able to come alone, I will bring a sketchbook like old times, and we will pass each other notes through brushstrokes and nods. No one will give me a second look in my drab calico dress. Only you know the colors of my heart.

–Your Muse

A Quilted Life

45

Trim away the fraying edges.
Square the corners of your memories.
Check the measurements
Against the pattern
Of life, they gave to you.

Stitch together timelines
Of who and where and what
Sew the blocks and stack them,
Organized by emotion.

Row by row,
We assemble, tying one to another:
Waves swirling over my toes, water clear as
glass, licking honey from my fingers and the last
remains of filo crumbs.
Potatoes frying in the kitchen where he made me
dinner, a recipe I still search for when there's
nothing else to eat.
The clatter of silverware on dishes, of glasses
raised in celebration, of another week conquered
as the opening credits roll.
Skating round in lazy laps to the music
requested by children's voices on Saturday
mornings as the disco ball spins.

Dancing in a circle, linked arm-in-arm with girls
in matching dresses, cheering as one takes the
first step into a fairy tale.
The stories devoured by eager eyes, reading to
escape the world for hours, coming up only long
enough to eat or grab tissues for the tears.
Weeping at the silence where there once was the
clatter of nails on tiled floors, where tails stirred
the air, waiting for another treat to fall.

Thread the needle, once again,
With the invisible strings.
Push it through the layers,
Binding,
Admiring,
The quilt you have sewn.

Escape

47

The world was peaceful,
Until she closed her book.

www.ingramcontent.com/pod-product-compliance
Lightning Source LLC
LaVergne TN
LVHW021253200726
843509LV00012B/1655